How to Crea

Mandalas

Jessica Mazurkiewicz

Dover Publications, Inc.
Mineola, New York

Bibliographical Note

How to Create Mandalas is a new work, first published by
Dover Publications, Inc., in 2013.

International Standard Book Number

ISBN-13: 978-0-486-49179-0
ISBN-10: 0-486-49179-X

Manufactured in the United States by RR Donnelley
49179X05   2016
www.doverpublications.com

Introduction

When drawing a mandala, it can be difficult to know where to begin. This book breaks down drawing a mandala into simple steps that will have you creating your own designs in no time.

Learning to draw your own personal mandalas is a wonderful way to relax and have fun. Many people find that the experience of creating a mandala helps them to learn about themselves and to meditate.

The exercises in this book will get you comfortable with making your own templates and creating symmetry in your mandalas. Don't get frustrated if your first mandalas aren't perfect. Each time you draw a mandala, it will become easier. The most important thing is to have fun!

Materials Needed

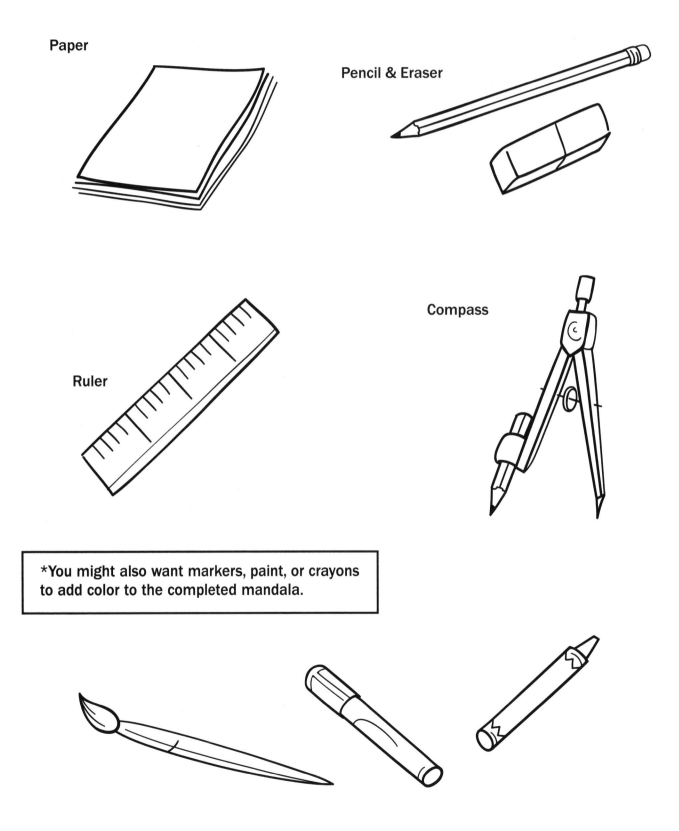

Paper

Pencil & Eraser

Ruler

Compass

*You might also want markers, paint, or crayons to add color to the completed mandala.

Create a Mandala Template

Step 1: Use your compass to lightly draw a circle the size you want your mandala to be.

Step 2: Find the small hole or indentation that the compass made in the center of your circle. Use it as a guide to draw a horizontal line going across the center, and a vertical line through the center. This will create four even areas.

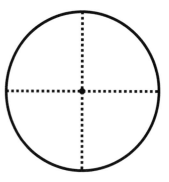

Tips

Draw the lines on the template lightly. You can erase them once the mandala is completed.

Don't worry if the template is not perfect. The more mandalas you draw, the easier this step will become.

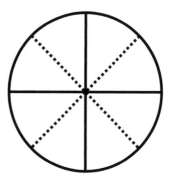

Step 3: Add two diagonal lines crossing the center of your circle. Try to make them at about 45 degrees so that the eight areas in your circle are all the same size.

Step 4: Use the compass to add smaller, evenly spaced circles to use as guides within your larger circle. This will complete your template.

Practice Making a Template

Here are some practice circles to get you started creating your own templates.

Use your ruler and pencil to draw the horizontal, vertical, and then diagonal lines.

Use your compass to add smaller circles within the template.

One has been filled in for you.

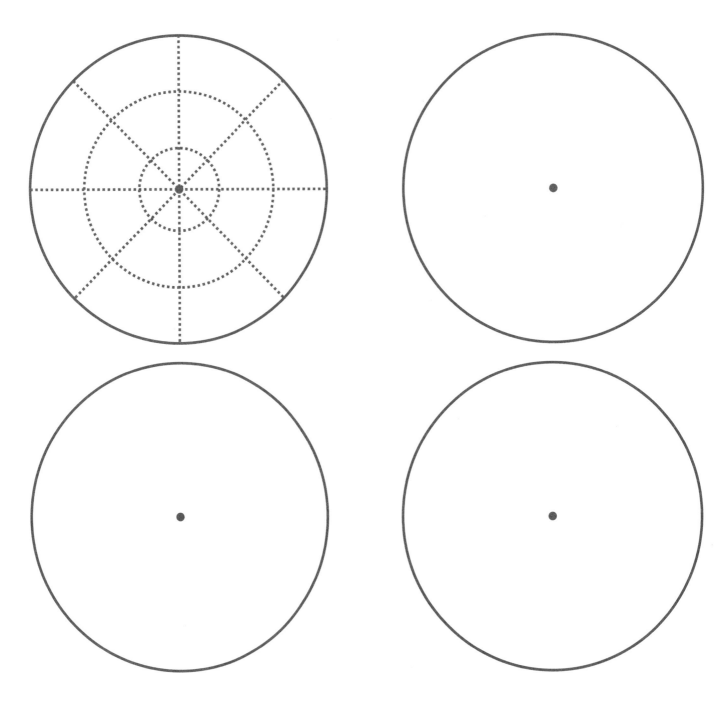

Inspiration Shapes For Your Mandala

Now that your template is completed you can begin drawing designs in your mandala. The shapes shown below will help get you started.

Don't feel limited to these shapes. Your favorite animals, plants, foods, letters, or numbers can make excellent elements in your mandalas.

Tips

There are no rules for creating your own mandala. Draw something you enjoy; you will be repeating the shape in each section of your mandala.

Repetition is key. If you draw a star in one part of your mandala, make sure to repeat it in the same area of each section.

Your shapes don't have to be complex. Simple elements such as lines, loops, circles, triangles, or diamonds can make a beautiful and meaningful mandala.

Begin to Draw Your Mandala

Step 1: Start by drawing a shape in the center of your template. A circle, flower, or star are some ideas.

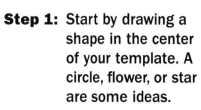

Tips

Use any drawing tool that you like to draw your mandala. Some people prefer to start drawing with pencil and then add marker or paint later on, and some people like to start with color right away.

The template lines can be erased as you go, or you can erase them at the end when your mandala is completed.

Take your time as you go around the circle drawing each element in the same area of each section of the circle.

Step 2: Add another shape or two outside the first shape.

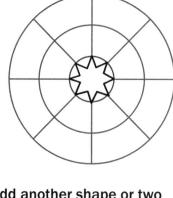

Step 3: Keep adding elements repeating around your mandala.

Step 4: As you continue to add more elements, experiment to create unique shapes. Shapes can overlap or detail can be added to an already drawn motif.

Step 5: Keep drawing until you feel your mandala is complete.

Follow 8 Steps to Complete Each Mandala

Fill the mandala elements into each section of the circle as shown in steps 1 through 8.

Use the guidelines in the template to help you draw each element in the same area of each section.

One mandala is shown below.

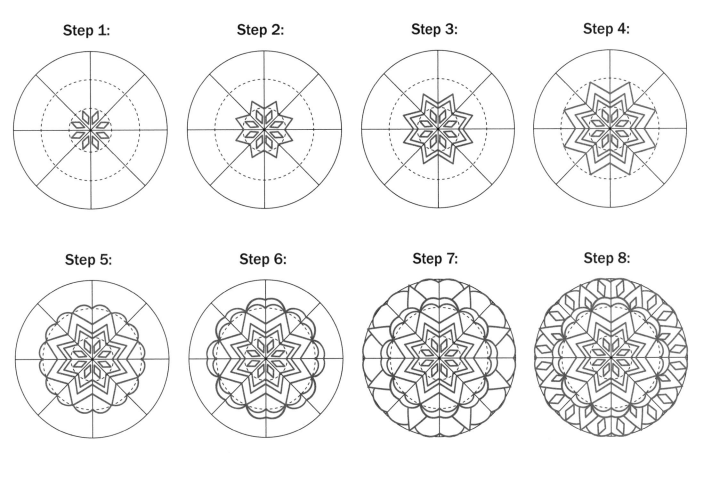

Step 1:   Step 2:   Step 3:   Step 4:

Step 5:   Step 6:   Step 7:   Step 8:

Step 1: **Step 2:** **Step 3:** **Step 4:**

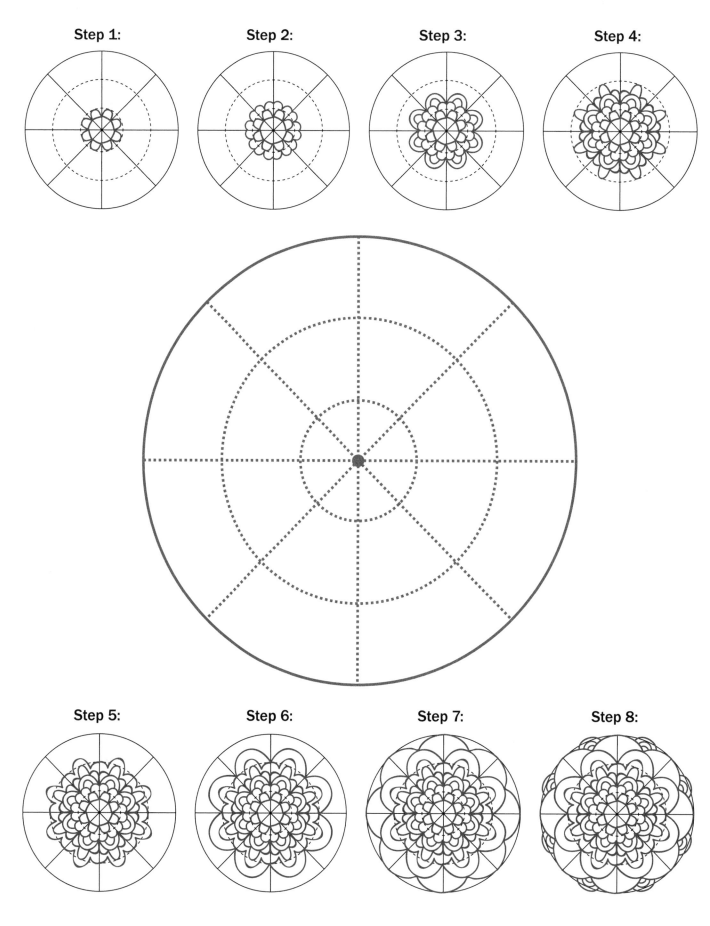

Step 5: **Step 6:** **Step 7:** **Step 8:**

Step 1: **Step 2:** **Step 3:** **Step 4:**

Step 5: **Step 6:** **Step 7:** **Step 8:**

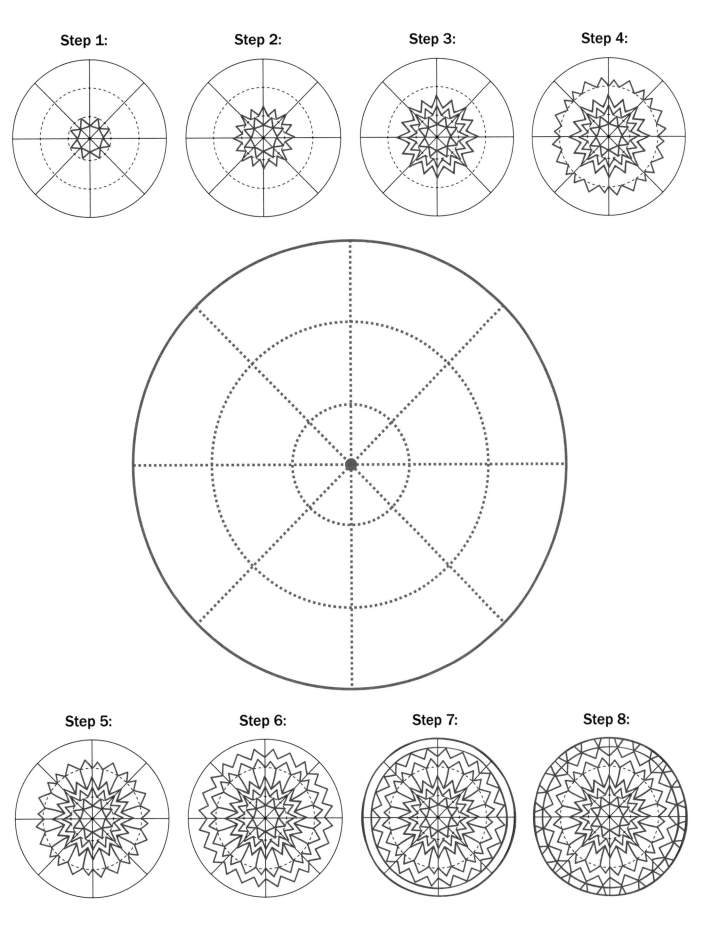

9

Step 1: Step 2: Step 3: Step 4:

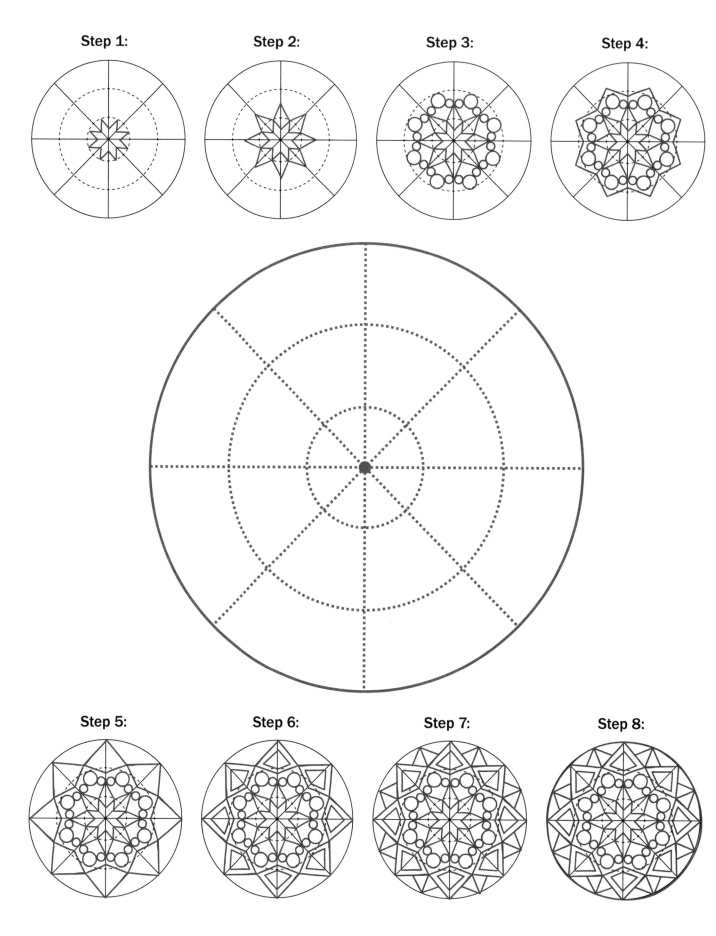

Step 5: Step 6: Step 7: Step 8:

Color the Mandalas

Adding color to the completed mandalas provided in this chapter will help you get a feel for creating your own.

Try to use the same colors on repeating shapes in each section to create symmetry and balance. This is an important element in a mandala.

Complete Half the Mandala

In this chapter, half of each mandala has been completed. Use what you have learned to complete the missing half.

If you need help getting started, try folding the page and placing it against a mirror to see its reflection. This will show you how the finished mandala will look.

18

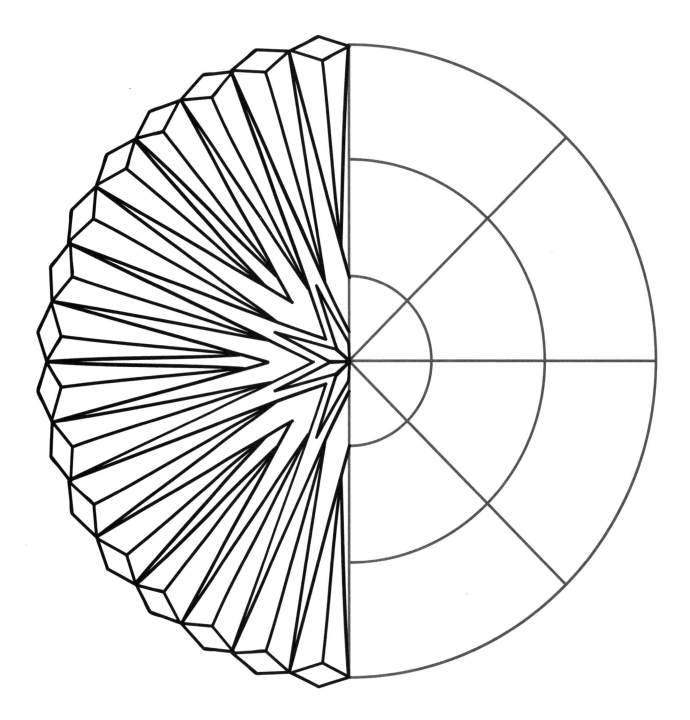

Fill in the Missing Sections

In this chapter, alternating sections of each mandala are provided.
Complete each mandala by repeating the design in the blank sections.

Try starting near the center, working your way toward the outer edge as
you draw each element of the design.

If you want an additional challenge, make up your own original design
and repeat it in each blank section, instead of copying the provided art.
This will create an asymmetrical mandala like the one in the lower example.

Repeat the Mandala Elements

In this chapter, one part of the mandala is provided in each section of the circle. Repeat each element in the same area of the other seven sections to create a complete mandala.

If you are having trouble getting started, begin by drawing the centermost element and working your way toward the outer edges of the circle from there.

The figures below illustrate how the individual elements will combine to create a complete mandala.

Complete the Mandalas, Part 1

Some elements have been provided in each mandala in this chapter.

Complete the mandala by adding more elements. Draw some shapes on the directional lines, and some shapes between the lines. Feel free to repeat elements, and introduce new ones as you go.

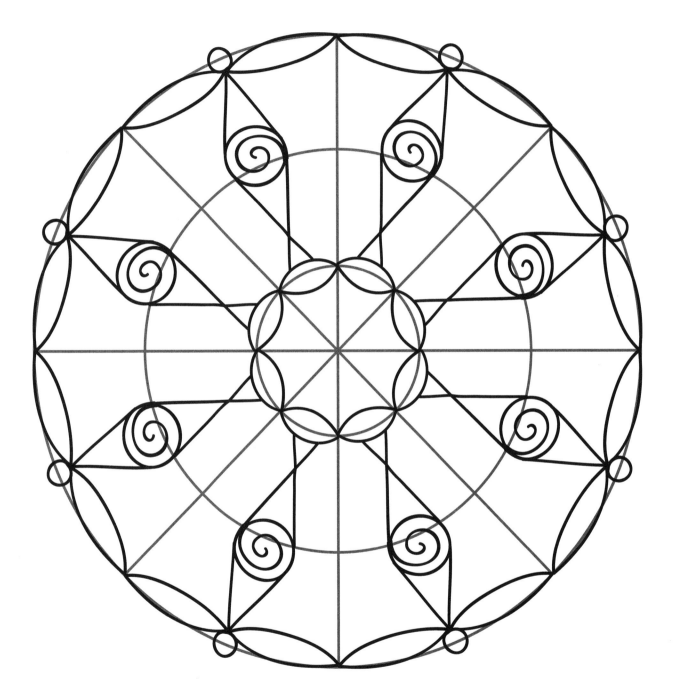

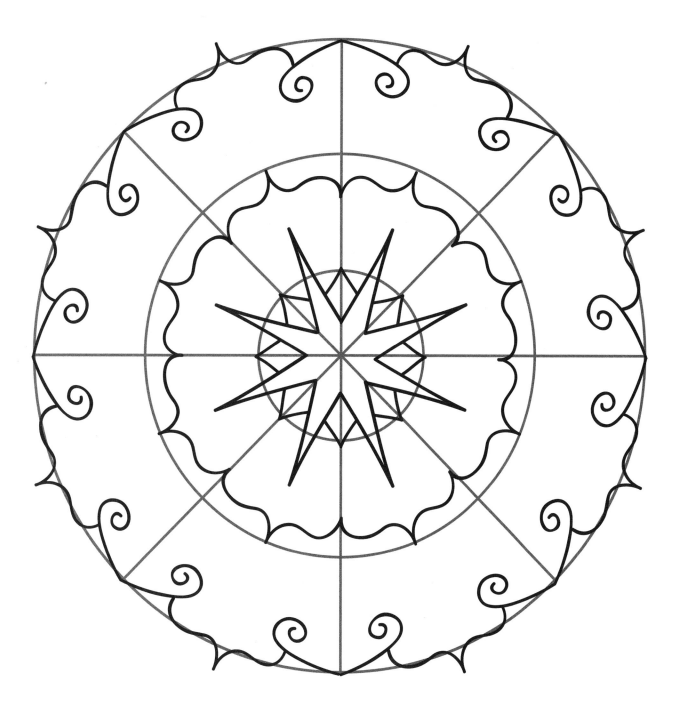

Complete the Mandalas, Part 2

By now you should be getting very comfortable drawing mandalas. The mandalas in this chapter have been started in the center.

Finish each mandala by adding whatever elements you desire. Remember that the mandala is a circle shape, but the outer edge does not have to be a perfect circle. You can line the outer edge of your mandala with any elements you enjoy drawing.

You can choose to add additional elements to the center of each mandala for a more complex design.